# HTML and CSS Beginners Guide

Navigating the Digital Frontier - Vision,
Development, Coding, and Designing the Web

## James Hammock

# CONTENTS

Introduction.............................................5


CHAPTER 1:Introduction to HTML and CSS...........7

Brief overview of HTML and CSS.....................…..…9

Importance and role in web development..............11


CHAPTER 2:Getting Started with HTML…..........14

Structure of an HTML document…....................18

HTML tags, elements, and attributes..................22

Creating headings, paragraphs, and lists...............26


CHAPTER 3:Understanding CSS.....................30

Introduction to CSS and its purpose...................34

CSS syntax and how to apply styles...................37

Selectors, properties, and values....................…..42


CHAPTER 4:Styling with CSS......................46

Colors, fonts, and text properties.....................…..52

Backgrounds and borders............................58

Box model and spacing................................63

CHAPTER 5:Layout and Positioning...................**68**

Block vs. inline elements..............................**75**

Positioning elements using CSS........................**79**

Layout techniques: flexbox and grid...................**85**


CHAPTER 6:Responsive Web Design..................**90**

Introduction to responsive design.....................**94**

Media queries for different devices.....................**96**

Making a webpage mobile-friendly.....................**100**


CHAPTER 7:Project: Build a Simple Webpage........**105**

Step-by-step guide to creating a basic webpage........**109**

Incorporating HTML and CSS to style the webpage...**114**


CHAPTER 8:Tips and Best Practices...................**119**

Proper indentation and code organization.............**124**

Cross-browser compatibility...........................**131**

Accessibility considerations...........................**135**


Conclusion...........................................**141**

# INTRODUCTION

Welcome to the Beginner's Guide to HTML and CSS, your gateway to the fascinating world of web development! HTML (HyperText Markup Language) and CSS (Cascading Style Sheets) are the foundational building blocks of virtually every website on the internet. HTML provides the structure and content of a webpage, while CSS dictates its visual style and layout. As a beginner, understanding these languages is essential for creating appealing and functional web pages.

Imagine you're embarking on a journey to construct your own digital masterpiece. With HTML, you'll wield tags to define headings, paragraphs, images, and links, allowing you to structure your content effectively. It's like crafting the framework of a house, arranging rooms and corridors.

Now, picture adding colors, choosing fonts, and arranging furniture in that house. This is where CSS steps in, allowing you to style your website to your heart's content. You'll apply CSS rules to give your webpage its unique personality, akin to painting the walls, arranging furniture, and deciding on the decor.

Throughout this guide, we'll unravel the mysteries of HTML and CSS, walking hand-in-hand through tutorials and examples. Together, we'll build the foundation for your web development journey, unlocking the potential to create and design your corner of the internet. Let's get started on this exciting path of coding and creativity!

# CHAPTER 1:Introduction to HTML and CSS

Welcome to the exciting world of web development with HTML and CSS! These two essential languages are the bedrock of every webpage you see on the internet. Let's dive into what makes them so vital.

HTML, which stands for HyperText Markup Language, provides the structural foundation of a webpage. Think of it as the framework of a house; it defines the basic structure, such as headings, paragraphs, images, and links. HTML uses tags, like <head>, <body>, <p>, and <img>, to organize and present content.

On the other hand, CSS, or Cascading Style Sheets, adds the visual appeal and layout to your HTML structure. It's like the interior design of your house, determining colors, fonts, spacing, and positioning.

CSS allows you to create a cohesive and aesthetically pleasing design for your website.

Mastering HTML and CSS opens doors to creating captivating websites and understanding how the digital world is constructed. In this guide, we'll start from the ground up, exploring the basics, syntax, and best practices to help you craft visually appealing and functionally sound web pages. Whether you're a complete beginner or looking to enhance your skills, let's embark on this coding journey and bring your web design visions to life!

# Brief overview of HTML and CSS

HTML (HyperText Markup Language) and CSS (Cascading Style Sheets) are fundamental languages for web development.

**HTML:** HTML is the backbone of web content. It uses markup tags to define the structure and elements of a webpage, such as headings, paragraphs, lists, links, images, and more. It provides the necessary scaffolding to organize information and present it on a browser.

**CSS:** CSS complements HTML by controlling the presentation and layout of web content. It allows developers to style HTML elements, specifying aspects like colors, fonts, spacing, and positioning. CSS ensures a visually appealing and consistent design across various devices and screen sizes.

Together, HTML and CSS form the basis for creating engaging and user-friendly websites. By combining the structure defined by HTML with the styling capabilities of CSS, developers can craft well-designed web pages that captivate users and deliver a seamless browsing experience.

Understanding and mastering these two languages is crucial for anyone aspiring to build, design, or modify web content. As you delve deeper into web development, you'll uncover the true potential of HTML and CSS, enabling you to create stunning, responsive, and interactive websites.

# Importance and role in web development

HTML (HyperText Markup Language) and CSS (Cascading Style Sheets) play critical roles in web development, forming the foundation of creating visually appealing, structured, and interactive websites.

**1. Structure and Content (HTML):** HTML is the backbone of a webpage, defining its structure and content. It lays the groundwork by organizing elements like headings, paragraphs, lists, links, forms, and multimedia. Without HTML, websites would lack structure and readability.

**2. Visual Styling (CSS):** CSS complements HTML by controlling the layout and presentation of the webpage. It allows developers to style HTML elements, determining colors, fonts, spacing, and positioning. This separation of content (HTML) and presentation (CSS) enhances maintainability and flexibility in web design.

**3. Cross-Device Compatibility:** HTML and CSS enable developers to create websites that are responsive and compatible with various devices, including desktops, tablets, and smartphones. CSS's media queries, for instance, help adapt layouts to different screen sizes, ensuring a seamless user experience.

**4. User Experience and Accessibility:** Well-structured HTML and thoughtful CSS design contribute to a positive user experience. Clear organization and intuitive design enhance navigation, while accessible design practices ensure that websites are usable by all, including those with disabilities.

5. Search Engine Optimization (SEO): Properly structured HTML, combined with CSS, contributes to better SEO. Search engines can easily crawl and index well-organized HTML content, while CSS

optimization improves load times, positively impacting search rankings.

**6. Dynamic Web Applications:** HTML and CSS are foundational for building dynamic web applications. When combined with JavaScript, HTML and CSS allow developers to create interactive and engaging user interfaces, providing rich user experiences.

In essence, HTML and CSS are the building blocks that empower developers to create aesthetically pleasing, functional, and accessible websites. Mastering these languages is fundamental for anyone pursuing a career in web development, enabling them to design and develop websites that meet modern user expectations and industry standards.

# CHAPTER 2:Getting Started with HTML

Getting started with HTML is an exciting first step into the world of web development. Here's a beginner-friendly guide to help you begin:

## 1. Understand the Basics:

- HTML stands for HyperText Markup Language. It uses markup tags enclosed in angle brackets (<>) to define elements.
- Elements are building blocks like headings, paragraphs, links, images, lists, etc.
- A basic HTML structure includes the `<html>`, `<head>`, and `<body>` elements.

## 2. Setting Up Your Environment:

- Open a text editor like Visual Studio Code, Sublime Text, or Notepad.
- Save your file with a ".html" extension, for example, "index.html".

# 3. Creating Your First HTML Page:

- Start with the basic structure:

```html
<!DOCTYPE html>
<html>
  <head>
    <title>Your Title</title>
  </head>
  <body>
    <h1>Hello, World!</h1>
  </body>
</html>
```

# 4. Understanding Tags:

- Tags are used to define elements. They are opened with `<tag>` and closed with `</tag>`.
- `<h1>` is a tag for the main heading. The numbers indicate the heading level (1 being the highest).

## 5. Adding Content:

- Experiment with different elements and their attributes.
- Use tags like `<p>` for paragraphs, `<a>` for links, `<img>` for images, and more.

## 6. Styling with CSS:

- You can add CSS within a `<style>` tag in the head or link an external CSS file.
- Example using an internal style:

```html
<head>
  <style>
    h1 {
        color: blue;
    }
  </style>
</head>
```

## 7. Testing Your Page:

- Open the HTML file in a web browser (e.g., Chrome, Firefox) to see the rendered output.

## 8. Further Learning:

- Explore online tutorials, courses, and resources to deepen your understanding of HTML.
- Learn about more HTML elements, attributes, forms, tables, and semantic HTML.

Practice, experimentation, and building small projects will help solidify your understanding of HTML. As you progress, you'll learn to create complex and visually appealing web pages. Good luck on your HTML learning journey!

# Structure of an HTML document

The structure of an HTML document is a fundamental framework that every webpage follows. It consists of several key elements that organize content and define essential properties. Here's a breakdown of a typical HTML document structure:

```html
<!DOCTYPE html>
<html>
<head>
  <title>Your Title</title>
  <!-- Meta tags, links to stylesheets, and other head elements -->
</head>
<body>
  <!-- Content of the webpage goes here -->
  <header>
    <!-- Header content: logo, navigation, etc. -->
  </header>
```

```
    <main>
        <!-- Main content of the webpage -->
        <section>
            <!-- A section of content -->
        </section>

        <article>
            <!-- An independent piece of content, like a
blog post -->
        </article>
    </main>

    <footer>
        <!-- Footer content: copyright, links, etc. -->
    </footer>
</body>
</html>
```

# Explanation of the structure:

**1.** `<!DOCTYPE html>`: Declaration indicating the version of HTML being used (HTML5 in this case).

**2.** `<html>`: The root element, encapsulating the entire HTML content.

**3.** `<head>`: Contains meta-information about the document, such as title, links to stylesheets, and more.

**4.** `<title>`: Sets the title of the webpage, displayed in the browser's title bar or tab.

**5.** `<body>`: Contains the visible content of the webpage, including text, images, links, and other elements.

**6.** `<header>`: Typically includes introductory content like logos, navigation menus, and headings.

**7.** `<main>`: Encloses the main content of the webpage, often comprising various sections and articles.

**8.** `<section>`: Defines a thematic grouping of content within the main section.

**9.** `<article>`: Represents an independent piece of content that makes sense on its own, like a blog post or news article.

**10.** `<footer>`: Typically includes information like copyright, links to related pages, and other footer-related content.

This structured organization enhances readability, accessibility, and maintenance of the webpage. As you delve deeper into HTML, you'll learn to use additional elements and attributes to create more complex and engaging web pages.

# HTML tags, elements, and attributes

Understanding HTML tags, elements, and attributes is fundamental to working with HTML. Let's break down each of these:

## 1. HTML Tags:

- HTML tags are the building blocks of HTML documents.
- Tags are enclosed in angle brackets (< >).
- Tags usually come in pairs: an opening tag and a closing tag.
- Example: `<tagname>content</tagname>`

## 2. HTML Elements:

- An HTML element consists of an opening tag, content, and a closing tag (when applicable).
- Elements are the basic structural units in HTML, representing different parts of a webpage.
- Example: `<p>Hello, this is a paragraph.</p>`

## 3. HTML Attributes:

- HTML attributes provide additional information about an element.
- Attributes are always specified in the opening tag.
- Attributes have a name and a value, separated by an equals sign.
- Example:

`<a href="https://example.com">Click here</a>`

**Let's explore a few commonly used HTML tags and their purposes:**

- `<html>`: Defines the root of an HTML document.
- `<head>`: Contains meta-information about the document.
- `<title>`: Sets the title of the webpage (displayed in the browser).
- `<body>`: Contains the visible content of the webpage.
- `<h1>, <h2>, ..., <h6>`: Heading tags, defining

headings of different levels.

- `<p>`: Represents a paragraph of text.
- `<a>`: Creates hyperlinks to other web pages or resources.
- `<img>`: Embeds images into the webpage.
- `<ul>, <ol>, <li>`: Defines unordered and ordered lists with list items.
- `<table>, <tr>, <th>, <td>`: Creates tables and their respective components (rows, headers, cells).

**For instance:**

```html
<!DOCTYPE html>
<html>
<head>
  <title>My Webpage</title>
</head>
<body>
  <h1>Welcome to My Webpage</h1>
```

```
    <p>This is a paragraph of text.</p>
    <a   href="https://example.com">Click   here   to
visit Example</a>
    <img    src="image.jpg"    alt="A    descriptive
image">
    <ul>
        <li>Item 1</li>
        <li>Item 2</li>
    </ul>
</body>
</html>
```

In this example, we have headings, a paragraph, a hyperlink, an image, and a simple list. Understanding and utilizing these HTML tags, elements, and attributes will enable you to create well-structured and functional web pages.

# Creating headings, paragraphs, and lists

Creating headings, paragraphs, and lists in HTML is relatively straightforward using specific HTML tags. Here's how you can create each of these elements:

## 1. Headings (`<h1>` to `<h6>`):

- HTML provides six levels of headings, ranging from `<h1>` for the main heading to `<h6>` for the least prominent.
- Use these tags to structure your content and provide hierarchy.

```html
<!DOCTYPE html>
<html>
<head>
    <title>Heading and Paragraph Example</title>
</head>
<body>
```

```html
    <h1>This is a Heading Level 1</h1>
    <h2>This is a Heading Level 2</h2>
    <h3>This is a Heading Level 3</h3>
    <h4>This is a Heading Level 4</h4>
    <h5>This is a Heading Level 5</h5>
    <h6>This is a Heading Level 6</h6>
</body>
</html>
```

## 2. Paragraphs (`<p>`):

- Use the `<p>` tag to define paragraphs of text.

```html
<!DOCTYPE html>
<html>
<head>
    <title>Heading and Paragraph Example</title>
</head>
<body>
    <p>This is a paragraph of text. It provides structure and readability to the content.</p>
```

```html
    <p>Another paragraph to demonstrate the use of
<strong>paragraphs</strong>.</p>
</body>
</html>
```

## 3. Lists (Ordered and Unordered):

- Use `<ul>` for an unordered (bulleted) list and `<ol>` for an ordered (numbered) list.
- List items are defined using the `<li>` (list item) tag within the `<ul>` or `<ol>`.

```html
<!DOCTYPE html>
<html>
<head>
  <title>List Example</title>
</head>
<body>
  <ul>
    <li>Item 1</li>
    <li>Item 2</li>
```

```
    <li>Item 3</li>
  </ul>

  <ol>
    <li>First item</li>
    <li>Second item</li>
    <li>Third item</li>
  </ol>
</body>
</html>
```
```

Feel free to mix and match these elements within your HTML document to create well-structured and readable content. Each element serves a specific purpose in organizing and presenting information on a webpage.
```

# CHAPTER 3:

# Understanding CSS

CSS (Cascading Style Sheets) is a stylesheet language used to control the presentation and layout of HTML documents. It allows you to style HTML elements and define how they should look on a web page. Here's a beginner-friendly understanding of CSS:

## 1. CSS Syntax:

- CSS uses a selector and a declaration block to style elements.
- The selector targets the HTML element you want to style.
- The declaration block contains one or more property-value pairs, defining the style.

```css
selector {
    property: value;
}
```

## 2. CSS Properties:

- CSS properties dictate the appearance and behavior of HTML elements.
- Examples include `color`, `font-size`, `margin`, `padding`, `background-color`, etc.

## 3. CSS Values:

- Values are assigned to properties and define specific styles.
- Examples: `color: red;`, `font-size: 16px;`, `margin: 10px;`.

## 4. Using Classes and IDs:

- Classes and IDs are attributes added to HTML elements to apply styles.
- Classes: `class="classname"`; multiple

elements can have the same class.

- IDs: `id="uniqueid"`; each ID should be unique.

## 5. Selectors:

- Selectors target elements to apply styles.
- Examples: `h1` targets all `<h1>` elements, `.classname` targets elements with a specific class, `#uniqueid` targets an element with a specific ID.

## 6. CSS Rules:

- A CSS rule is a combination of a selector and a declaration block.
- Multiple rules can be combined to style various elements.

```css
h1 {
    color: blue;
    font-size: 24px;
}
```

```
.classname {
    background-color: gray;
}
```
```

## 7. Applying CSS:

- CSS can be applied inline, internally, or externally.
- Inline: Directly within HTML elements using the `style` attribute.
- Internal: Inside the `<style>` element in the HTML `<head>`.
- External: In a separate CSS file linked to the HTML file using `<link>`.

## 8. Inheritance and Specificity:

- CSS styles can be inherited from parent elements to their children.
- Specificity defines which styles take precedence when multiple conflicting styles are applied.
```

## 9. Box Model:

- The box model consists of content, padding, border, and margin around an element.
- Understanding this helps in controlling element spacing and layout.

CSS is a powerful tool that enables you to create visually appealing and user-friendly websites. As you learn and practice, you'll gain proficiency in crafting elegant and responsive designs for your web projects.

# Introduction to CSS and its purpose

CSS, which stands for Cascading Style Sheets, is a fundamental technology in web development that plays a crucial role in shaping the appearance and layout of websites. It works alongside HTML to enhance the presentation of web pages by styling the content defined in HTML documents.

# Purpose of CSS:

## 1. Style and Presentation:

CSS is primarily used to style web content, allowing designers and developers to control the visual aspects of a webpage. This includes defining colors, fonts, spacing, layout, and more.

## 2. Separation of Concerns:

CSS promotes the separation of content (defined in HTML) and its presentation. This separation makes code more organized, maintainable, and easier to manage, especially in large-scale web development projects.

## 3. Reusability and Consistency:

By defining styles in one central location, CSS allows for the reuse of styles across multiple elements or even entire websites. This ensures a consistent and cohesive look and feel throughout the site.

## 4. Responsive Design:

CSS enables the creation of responsive designs that adapt to different screen sizes and devices. Through techniques like media queries and flexible layouts, CSS ensures that websites are accessible and visually appealing on various platforms.

## 5. Accessibility and User Experience:

Proper use of CSS contributes to a better user experience by making websites more accessible to all users, including those with disabilities. CSS allows for adjustments like text size and color contrast, enhancing readability and usability.

## 6. Performance Optimization:

Optimized CSS contributes to faster page loading times, which is crucial for a positive user experience. Properly structured and minimized CSS files reduce the amount of data that needs to be transferred to the user's browser.

In essence, CSS is the tool that brings web pages to life, making them visually appealing, functional, and accessible to a wide audience. Understanding how to utilize CSS effectively is essential for anyone involved in web development, whether they're designing the look of a website or creating a seamless user interface.

# CSS syntax and how to apply styles

CSS has a straightforward syntax that involves selectors, properties, and values. Let's break down the CSS syntax and how to apply styles:

## 1. CSS Syntax:

- CSS is made up of rules, each containing a selector and a declaration block.
- The selector specifies which HTML elements the style applies to.
- The declaration block contains one or more property-value pairs separated by semicolons.
- Properties define the style attribute (e.g., color,

font-size).

- Values are assigned to properties and specify the style (e.g., red, 16px).

```css
selector {
  property: value;
}
```

## 2. CSS Selectors:

- CSS selectors target HTML elements to apply styles.
- Selectors can be HTML tags, classes, IDs, attributes, and more.
- Multiple selectors can be grouped together with commas.

```css
h1 {
    color: blue;
}

.button {
    background-color: green;
}

#header {
    font-size: 24px;
}
```

## 3. Applying Styles:

- Styles can be applied inline, internally, or externally.
- Inline styles are applied directly to HTML elements using the `style` attribute.
- Internal styles are defined within the `<style>` element in the HTML `<head>`.
- External styles are in a separate CSS file

linked to the HTML file using `<link>`.

**Inline Styles:**

```html
<p style="color: red;">This is a paragraph with inline style.</p>
```

**Internal Styles:**

```html
<head>
  <style>
    h2 {
        font-size: 20px;
    }

    .box {
        border: 2px solid black;
    }
  </style>
</head>
```

**External Styles:**

```html
<head>
  <link rel="stylesheet" href="styles.css">
</head>
```

In this example, "styles.css" is an external CSS file containing CSS rules.

Understanding and utilizing CSS syntax allows you to style HTML elements, making your web pages visually appealing and user-friendly. The flexibility of CSS helps achieve consistent designs, responsive layouts, and enhanced user experiences across various devices.

# Selectors, properties, and values

Understanding selectors, properties, and values is crucial for effectively using CSS to style HTML elements. Let's explore each of these components in detail:

## 1. Selectors:

**Definition:** Selectors are patterns used to select and style HTML elements.

**Purpose:** Selectors target specific elements to apply styles, allowing for precise control over appearance.

**Examples:**

- **Tag Selector:** `p` selects all `<p>` paragraphs.
- **Class Selector:** `.classname` selects elements with a specific class, e.g., `<div class="box">`.
- **ID Selector:** `#uniqueid` selects an element with a unique ID, e.g., `<div id="header">`.
- **Attribute Selector:** `[attribute=value]`

selects elements with a specific attribute and value, e.g., `<a href="example.com">`.

## 2. Properties:

**Definition:** Properties are the style attributes applied to selected elements.

**Purpose:** Properties define the visual presentation of the elements, such as color, size, margin, padding, etc.

**Examples:**

- `color`: Sets the color of the text.
- `font-size`: Defines the size of the font.
- `background-color`: Sets the background color of an element.
- `margin`: Controls the spacing outside the element.
- `padding`: Controls the spacing inside the element.

## 3. Values:

**Definition:** Values are assigned to properties and determine how the style is applied.

**Purpose:** Values customize the appearance by specifying colors, sizes, positions, etc.

**Examples:**

- `color: red;` sets the text color to red.
- `font-size: 16px;` sets the font size to 16 pixels.
- `background-color: #00ff00;` sets the background color to green (hexadecimal color value).
- `margin: 10px 20px;` sets a top and bottom margin of 10 pixels and left and right margin of 20 pixels.

Putting it all together, here's an example CSS rule using a selector, property, and value:

```css
/* Selector: targets all h1 elements */
h1 {
    /* Property: sets the color of the text */
    color: blue;
    /* Property: sets the font size */
    font-size: 24px;
```

```
}
```
```
```

In this example, the selector `h1` targets all `<h1>` elements, and the properties `color` and `font-size` define their appearance using the specified values.

Mastering the usage of selectors, properties, and values allows you to craft styles that make your web pages visually appealing and engaging for users.

# CHAPTER 4:Styling with CSS

Styling with CSS involves applying styles to HTML elements to enhance their appearance and layout. Here are the key steps and techniques for effective styling:

## 1. CSS Syntax:

- CSS uses a selector, followed by a declaration block containing properties and values.
- Multiple properties and values are separated by semicolons within the declaration block.
- Example:

```css
selector {
    property1: value1;
    property2: value2;
    /* more properties and values */
}
```

## 2. Using Selectors:

- Target elements using various selectors (tags, classes, IDs, attributes) to apply styles.
- Combine selectors for more specific targeting.
- Example:

```css
/* Tag Selector */
h1 {
    font-size: 24px;
}

/* Class Selector */
.box {
    background-color: lightgray;
}

/* ID Selector */
#header {
    font-family: "Arial", sans-serif;
}
```

## 3. Applying Properties and Values:

- Use properties to define specific styles like color, font-size, padding, margin, etc.
- Assign values to properties to specify the style details.
- Example:

```css
/* Setting color and background color */
p {
    color: blue;
    background-color: yellow;
}

/* Defining padding and margin */
.box {
    padding: 10px;
    margin: 20px;
}
```

## 4. Using Shorthand Properties:

- Shorthand properties allow you to set multiple related properties in a single line.
- Example:

```css
/* Shorthand for margin: top right bottom left; */
.box {
    margin: 10px 20px 10px 5px;
}
```

## 5. CSS Classes and IDs:

- Assign styles to HTML elements using class and ID selectors.
- Classes can be applied to multiple elements, while IDs should be unique.
- Example:

```css
/* Applying style to a class */
.highlight {
```

```css
    font-weight: bold;
    color: red;
}


/* Applying style to an ID */
#header {
    background-color: lightgray;
}
```

## 6. External CSS:

- For maintainability, place CSS in a separate external file (e.g., `styles.css`).
- Link the external CSS file in the HTML using `<link>` within the `<head>` section.
- Example:

```html
<head>
    <link rel="stylesheet" href="styles.css">
</head>
```

# 7. CSS Specificity:

- CSS follows a specificity hierarchy to determine which styles to apply when conflicting rules exist.
- Be aware of this hierarchy to control the styling accurately.
- Example:

```css
/* Specificity example */
.box {
    color: blue;
}

div.box {
    color: red;
}
```

By utilizing these techniques and principles, you can style your web content effectively, creating visually appealing and user-friendly webpages. Experiment with various styles and selectors to achieve the desired look and feel for your website.

# Colors, fonts, and text properties

Styling text with colors, fonts, and various text properties is a significant aspect of CSS. Here's a guide on how to apply styles to text:

**1. Color (color):**
   - Use the `color` property to set the text color.
   - Colors can be specified using names, hex codes, rgb values, or rgba values.
   - Example:

```css
/* Using color names */
p {
    color: red;
```

```css
}

/* Using hex code */
h1 {
    color: #00ff00; /* Green */
}

/* Using rgb value */
.box {
    color: rgb(255, 0, 0); /* Red */
}

/* Using rgba value for transparency */
.transparent-text {
    color: rgba(0, 0, 255, 0.5);
/* Semi-transparent blue */
}
```
```

## 2. Fonts (font-family, font-size):

- Use the `font-family` property to set the font of the text.
```

- Use the `font-size` property to set the size of the font.
- Fonts should be specified in a fallback sequence in case a font is not available.
- Example:

```css
/* Setting font-family with fallbacks */
p {
    font-family: Arial, sans-serif; /* Arial as the primary font, sans-serif as fallback */
}

/* Setting font size */
h2 {
    font-size: 24px;
}
```

## 3. Font Weight (font-weight):

- Use the `font-weight` property to set the thickness of the characters in the text.

- Values include normal, bold, bolder, lighter, or numerical values (100 to 900).
- Example:

```css
/* Setting font weight */
.bold-text {
    font-weight: bold;
}

.light-text {
    font-weight: lighter;
}
```

## 4. Text Alignment (text-align):

- Use the `text-align` property to control the alignment of the text within its container.
- Values include left, right, center, and justify.
- Example:

```css
/* Setting text alignment */
.centered-text {
    text-align: center;
}
```

## 5. Text Decoration (text-decoration):

- Use the `text-decoration` property to add
  decoration to text, such as underline, overline,
  or line-through.
- Example:

```css
/* Adding underline to links */
a {
    text-decoration: underline;
}
```

# 6. Text Transform (text-transform):

- Use the `text-transform` property to control the capitalization of the text.
- Values include uppercase, lowercase, and capitalize.
- Example:

```css
/* Transforming text to uppercase */
.uppercase-text {
    text-transform: uppercase;
}
```

By utilizing these properties, you can style text in various ways to make it visually appealing and align with the design aesthetics of your web page. Experiment with different values and combinations to achieve the desired text style.

# Backgrounds and borders

Styling backgrounds and borders using CSS is crucial for enhancing the visual appeal and layout of web elements. Here's a guide on how to apply styles to backgrounds and borders:

## 1. Background Color (background-color):

   - Use the `background-color` property to set the background color of an element.

   - Colors can be specified using names, hex codes, rgb values, or rgba values.

   - Example:

```css
/* Setting background color using color names */
.box {
    background-color: lightgray;
}

/* Setting background color using hex code */
.highlight-box {
```

```css
    background-color: #ffcc00; /* Yellow */
}

/* Setting background color using rgb value */
.custom-background {
    background-color: rgb(100, 150, 200);
    /* A shade of blue */
}
```

## 2. Background Image (background-image):
- Use the `background-image` property to set a background image for an element.
- Use the `url()` function to specify the image file.
- Example:

```css
/* Setting a background image */
.bg-image {
    background-image: url('path/to/image.jpg');
}
```

```
```

## 3. Background Repeat (background-repeat):

- Use the `background-repeat` property to control how a background image is repeated.
- Values include repeat, repeat-x, repeat-y, and no-repeat.
- Example:

```css
/* Repeating the background image horizontally */
.bg-repeat {
    background-repeat: repeat-x;
}
```

## 4. Background Position (background-position):

- Use the `background-position` property to position a background image within its container.
- Values include keywords (left, right, top,

bottom) or percentages.

- Example:

```css
/* Positioning the background image at the top right corner */
.bg-position {
    background-position: top right;
}
```

## 5. Borders (border):

- Use the `border` property to set the border of an element.
- The `border` property can take values for width, style, and color.
- Example:

```css
/* Setting a 2px solid black border */
.bordered-box {
    border: 2px solid black;
```

```
}
```

## 6. Border Radius (border-radius):

- Use the `border-radius` property to create
  rounded corners for an element's border.
- Values specify the radius for each corner (in
  pixels or percentages).
- Example:

```css
/* Creating rounded corners with a 10px radius */
.rounded-box {
    border-radius: 10px;
}
```

These properties offer versatility in styling backgrounds and borders, allowing you to customize the appearance of elements and improve the overall design of your web page. Experiment with different values to achieve the desired visual effect.

# Box model and spacing

Understanding the box model and managing spacing is crucial for creating well-structured layouts and designs in CSS. The CSS box model describes the space around and within an HTML element, defining how the element is displayed in terms of content area, padding, border, and margin.

## Here's a breakdown of the CSS box model components and how to manage spacing:

### 1. Content Area:
- The content area is where the actual content of the element (text, images, etc.) is displayed.
- Its size is set using properties like `width` and `height`.

### 2. Padding (padding):
- Padding is the space between the content area and the border.
- It helps create space around the content within

the element.

- Padding can be set for individual sides (top, right, bottom, left) or as a single value.
- Example:

```css
/* Setting padding for all sides */
.box {
    padding: 20px; /* Applies 20px padding to all sides */
}

/* Setting padding for individual sides */
.box {
    padding-top: 10px;
    padding-right: 15px;
    padding-bottom: 10px;
    padding-left: 15px;
}
```

## 3. Border (border):

- The border is a line that surrounds the padding and content area.
- It separates the element from its surrounding elements.
- Border properties include `border-width`, `border-style`, and `border-color`.
- Example:

```css
/* Setting a border */
.box {
    border: 2px solid black; /* 2px solid black border */
}
```

## 4. Margin (margin):

- Margin is the space outside the border, creating space between the element and neighboring elements.
- It helps control the layout and positioning of

elements on the page.

- Like padding, margin can be set for individual sides or as a single value.

- Example:

```css
/* Setting margin for all sides */
.box {
    margin: 10px; /* Applies 10px margin to all
      sides */
}

/* Setting margin for individual sides */
.box {
    margin-top: 10px;
    margin-right: 15px;
    margin-bottom: 10px;
    margin-left: 15px;
}
```

## 5. Box Model Visualization:

- The cumulative effect of content, padding, border, and margin can be visualized as follows:

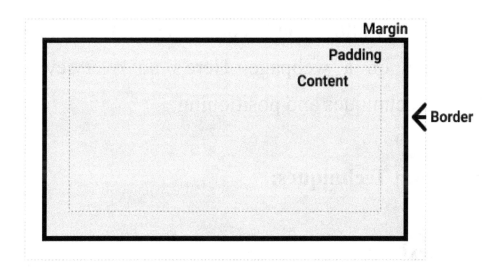

By manipulating these components of the box model, you can effectively control the spacing and layout of your web elements, creating a visually appealing and well-structured design for your web page. Experiment with different values for padding, border, and margin to achieve the desired layout and spacing.

# CHAPTER 5:Layout and Positioning

Layout and positioning in CSS are crucial for creating visually appealing and well-structured web pages. They allow you to control the arrangement of elements on a webpage. Here's an overview of layout techniques and positioning:

## 1. Layout Techniques:

### Flexbox:

- Flexbox is a one-dimensional layout method that allows you to arrange items within a container either horizontally or vertically.
- It provides properties like `display`, `flex-direction`, `justify-content`, `align-items`, etc., to control the layout.
- Flexbox is excellent for creating responsive and dynamic layouts.

**Example:**

```css
.flex-container {
    display: flex;
    flex-direction: row; /* or column for vertical layout */
    justify-content: space-between; /* or other alignment options */
    align-items: center;
}
```

**Grid:**
- CSS Grid is a two-dimensional layout system that allows you to create complex layouts with rows and columns.
- It provides properties like `display`, `grid-template-rows`, `grid-template-columns`, `grid-gap`, etc.
- Grid is powerful for creating symmetrical and responsive layouts.

**Example:**

```css
.grid-container {
    display: grid;
    grid-template-columns: 1fr 1fr 1fr; /* Three equal columns */
    grid-template-rows: auto; /* Auto-sized rows */
    grid-gap: 10px; /* Gap between grid items */
}
```

## 2. Positioning:

Relative Positioning (position: relative):
- Relative positioning moves an element relative to its normal position.
- The element remains in the normal document flow, and other elements are not affected.

- Use properties like `top`, `right`, `bottom`, `left` to position the element relative to its normal position.

**Example:**

```css
.relative-box {
    position: relative;
    top: 20px;
    left: 10px;
}
```

**Absolute Positioning (position: absolute):**

- Absolute positioning positions an element relative to its closest positioned ancestor (an ancestor with a position other than static).
- The element is taken out of the normal document flow.
- Use properties like `top`, `right`, `bottom`, `left` to position the element relative to its closest

positioned ancestor.

**Example:**

```css
.absolute-box {
    position: absolute;
    top: 50px;
    left: 30px;
}
```

**Fixed Positioning (position: fixed):**
- Fixed positioning positions an element relative to the viewport, even when the page is scrolled.
- The element is taken out of the normal document flow.
- Use properties like `top`, `right`, `bottom`, `left` to position the element relative to the viewport.

**Example:**

```css
.fixed-box {
    position: fixed;
    top: 0;
    right: 0;
}
```

**Sticky Positioning (position: sticky):**
   - Sticky positioning is a hybrid of relative and fixed positioning.
- The element is treated as relative positioned until it crosses a specified point, then it is treated as fixed positioned.
- Use the `top`, `right`, `bottom`, or `left` property to control when the element becomes "stuck".

**Example:**

```css
.sticky-box {
    position: sticky;
    top: 20px;
}
```

Understanding and utilizing these layout techniques and positioning methods in CSS will enable you to create flexible, dynamic, and visually appealing web layouts. Experiment with different properties and values to achieve the desired positioning and layout for your web page.

# Block vs. inline elements

In HTML and CSS, elements are categorized into two main types: block-level elements and inline elements. These types determine how elements are displayed in the browser and how they interact with other elements. Here's an overview of block and inline elements:

## 1. Block-Level Elements:

**Definition:** Block-level elements create a "block" or a rectangular box on the webpage, typically starting on a new line and stretching the full width available in the parent container.

Examples: `<div>`, `<p>`, `<h1>`, `<ul>`, `<li>`, `<table>`, `<form>`.

### Properties:

- They accept width, height, margin, padding, and border properties.
- By default, they take up the full available

width of their parent container.

```html
<div>
  <p>This is a block-level element.</p>
</div>
```

## 2. Inline Elements:

**Definition:** Inline elements do not create a new "block" and only take up as much width as necessary. They flow within the content and appear on the same line as much as possible.

**Examples:** `<span>`, `<a>`, `<strong>`, `<em>`, `<img>`, `<br>`.

## Properties:

- They don't accept width, height, margin, or padding properties for the top and bottom.
- They respect the width and height of their content.

```html
<p>This is an <span>inline element</span> within a paragraph.</p>
```

## 3. Different Use Cases:

- Use block-level elements for structural elements, grouping content, creating sections, or when you want elements to start on a new line.
- Use inline elements for styling, emphasizing specific parts of the text, or when you want elements to flow within the content.

## 4. Inline-Block Elements:

**Definition:** Inline-block elements are a hybrid, behaving like inline elements in terms of flow but allowing properties like width, height, margin, and padding.

**Examples:** `<span style="display: inline-block;">`, `<img>`, `<button>`.

**Properties:**

- They accept width, height, margin, padding, and border properties.

```html
<span style="display: inline-block;">
    This is an inline-block element.
</span>
```

Understanding the differences between block-level and inline elements is fundamental for creating the desired layout and structure in your HTML and CSS. Choose the appropriate type based on the behavior and appearance you want to achieve.

# Positioning elements using CSS

Positioning elements using CSS is essential for achieving precise layouts and controlling the placement of elements on a webpage. CSS provides several properties and techniques to position elements. Here are the commonly used positioning methods:

**1. Relative Positioning (`position: relative;`):**
- Elements with `position: relative;` are positioned relative to their normal position.
- Use `top`, `right`, `bottom`, and `left` properties to offset the element from its normal position.
- This technique does not remove the element from the document flow.

```css
.relative-box {
    position: relative;
    top: 20px;
```

```
    left: 10px;
}
```

## 2. Absolute Positioning (`position: absolute;`):

- Elements with `position: absolute;` are
  positioned relative to the nearest positioned
  ancestor (an ancestor with a position other than
  static).
- If there's no positioned ancestor, it's positioned
  relative to the document body.
- It's taken out of the normal document flow.
- Use `top`, `right`, `bottom`, and `left`
  properties to position the element.

```css
.absolute-box {
    position: absolute;
    top: 50px;
    left: 30px;
}
```

## 3. Fixed Positioning (`position: fixed;`):

- Elements with `position: fixed;` are positioned relative to the viewport (the browser window).
- They stay in the same place even if the page is scrolled.
- Use `top`, `right`, `bottom`, and `left` properties to position the element.

```css
.fixed-box {
    position: fixed;
    top: 0;
    right: 0;
}
```

## 4. Sticky Positioning (`position: sticky;`):

- Elements with `position: sticky;` are initially positioned according to the normal flow of the document.
- When the viewport crosses a specified point

(e.g., scrolling), it's treated as fixed.
- Useful for creating navigation bars that "stick" to the top as the user scrolls.

```css
.sticky-box {
    position: sticky;
    top: 20px;
}
```

## 5. Float (`float: left/right;`):

- The `float` property allows an element to be pushed to the left or right, allowing other content to wrap around it.
- Often used for creating a layout where text wraps around images.

```css
.float-left {
    float: left;
}
```

```css
.float-right {
    float: right;
}
```

## 6. Centering Elements:

- **Use `margin:** auto;` along with a defined `width` to horizontally center a block-level element within its parent.

```css
.centered-box {
    width: 50%; /* Or any width you desire */
    margin: auto;
}
```

## 7. Grid and Flexbox:

- Utilize CSS Grid and Flexbox for complex and responsive layouts. They provide powerful ways to position and align elements within a layout.

These positioning techniques empower you to create versatile layouts and achieve specific placement for elements on your webpage, enhancing the overall design and user experience. Experiment with these methods to achieve the desired positioning based on your design requirements.

# Layout techniques: flexbox and grid

Flexbox and Grid are two powerful layout techniques in CSS that allow for flexible and responsive design of web pages. Each has its unique advantages and use cases:

## 1. Flexbox:

**Definition:** Flexbox is a one-dimensional layout model that allows you to align and distribute items along a flex container in either a row or a column.

### Use Cases:
- Ideal for arranging items within a container in a single row or column, or a combination of both.
- Commonly used for navigation menus, forms, and flexible layouts.

**Key Properties:**

- \`display: flex;\` turns a container into a flex container.

- \`flex-direction: row|row-reverse|column|column-reverse;\` determines the direction of the main axis.

- \`justify-content: flex-start|flex-end|center|space-between|space-around;\` aligns items along the main axis.

- \`align-items: flex-start|flex-end|center|baseline|stretch;\` aligns items along the cross axis.

**Example:**

```css
.flex-container {
    display: flex;
    flex-direction: row; /* or column */
    justify-content: space-between;
    align-items: center;
}
```

## 2. Grid:

**Definition:** CSS Grid is a two-dimensional layout model that allows you to create a grid of rows and columns.

## Use Cases:

- Great for creating complex layouts with precise control over rows and columns.
- Useful for layouts where items need to span multiple rows or columns.

## Key Properties:

- `display: grid;` turns a container into a grid container.
- `grid-template-rows: <track-size>;` defines the height of the rows.
- `grid-template-columns: <track-size>;` defines the width of the columns.
- `grid-gap: <row-gap> <column-gap>;` defines the gap between rows and columns.
- `grid-row: <start-line> / <end-line>;` places

an item in a specific row.

- `grid-column: <start-line> / <end-line>;` places an item in a specific column.

**Example:**

```css
.grid-container {
    display: grid;
    grid-template-columns: 1fr 1fr 1fr; /* Three equal columns */
    grid-template-rows: auto; /* Auto-sized rows */
    grid-gap: 10px; /* Gap between grid items */
}
```

Both Flexbox and Grid layout techniques are immensely valuable for modern web development, allowing for efficient and responsive designs. Depending on the layout requirements, you can choose between them or even combine them to create intricate and dynamic layouts. Experimenting and mastering these techniques will greatly enhance your ability to design effective and visually appealing web interfaces.

# CHAPTER 6:Responsive Web Design

Responsive web design is an approach that aims to create web pages that adapt and display optimally across various devices and screen sizes. It ensures a seamless and consistent user experience regardless of whether the user is accessing the website on a desktop computer, tablet, smartphone, or other devices. Here are the key principles and techniques of responsive web design:

## 1. Fluid Grids:

- Design layouts using relative units like percentages instead of fixed units like pixels.
- Use flexible grids that scale with the screen size to create a fluid layout.

## 2. Flexible Images:

- Use CSS to ensure images resize proportionally to fit within their containing elements.

- Use the `max-width` property to prevent images from overflowing their containers.

## 3. Media Queries:

- Media queries are CSS techniques that apply styles based on the device's characteristics, such as screen width, height, or orientation.
- Adjust styles based on the device's screen size to create a responsive design.

```css
@media (max-width: 768px) {
    /* Styles for screens up to 768px width */
}


@media (min-width: 769px) and (max-width: 1200px) {
    /* Styles for screens between 769px and 1200px width */
}
```

# 4. Viewport Meta Tag:

- Use the viewport meta tag to control the viewport's width and scaling on mobile devices.
- Helps in rendering web content based on the device's screen size.

```html
<meta                          name="viewport" content="width=device-width, initial-scale=1.0">
```

# 5. CSS Frameworks:

- Utilize CSS frameworks like Bootstrap, Foundation, or Bulma that provide pre-built responsive grids and components.
- Speed up development by using predefined classes to create responsive designs.

## 6. Flexbox and CSS Grid:

- Employ Flexbox and CSS Grid layout techniques to create flexible and responsive layouts.
- These modern CSS features simplify the creation of complex and responsive designs.

## 7. Responsive Images:

- Use the `srcset` attribute to provide multiple image sources based on device pixel density or viewport width.
- Employ `picture` and `source` elements to serve appropriate images for different screen resolutions.

```html
<img          srcset="image-320w.jpg          320w,
image-480w.jpg 480w, image-800w.jpg 800w"
          sizes="(max-width:     320px)     280px,
(max-width: 480px) 440px, 800px"
          src="image-800w.jpg" alt="Description">
```

Responsive web design ensures that websites are accessible and usable across a wide range of devices, providing an enhanced user experience. By considering these principles and techniques, developers can create web designs that are flexible, adaptable, and visually appealing on various screen sizes.

# Introduction to responsive design

Responsive design is an approach to web development that emphasizes creating web pages that adjust and display seamlessly on various devices and screen sizes. This approach ensures that websites look and function well, providing an optimal user experience regardless of the device being used be it a desktop computer, laptop, tablet, smartphone, or even larger displays like TVs. The main goal is to accommodate the diverse ways users access web content in today's digital landscape.

The concept of responsive design is rooted in the understanding that the internet is accessed through a multitude of devices with varying screen dimensions and resolutions. As such, a one-size-fits-all approach to web design is no longer effective or user-friendly. Responsive design addresses this by employing flexible layouts, fluid grids, and intelligent use of CSS media queries.

Key principles of responsive design include using relative units, such as percentages and ems, instead of fixed units like pixels. This allows elements to scale and adapt based on the user's screen. Media queries are then employed to apply specific styles based on the device's characteristics, such as width, height, and orientation.

Furthermore, the use of flexible images and responsive typography ensures that content remains accessible and visually pleasing across different screen sizes. Modern CSS techniques, like Flexbox and CSS Grid, play a pivotal role in creating layouts that adapt to various screen dimensions.

In summary, responsive design is an essential approach in modern web development, promoting a seamless user experience by adapting web content to the specific device being used. By incorporating this approach, websites become more accessible, engaging, and functional across the vast array of devices available in today's digital ecosystem.

# Media queries for different devices

Media queries are a fundamental aspect of responsive web design, allowing you to apply specific styles based on the characteristics of the device or browser. By using media queries, you can create a responsive layout that adjusts to different screen sizes, resolutions, and orientations. Here are examples of media queries for targeting various devices:

# 1. Targeting Small Devices (Smartphones):

```css
@media (max-width: 767px) {
/* Styles for smartphones and smaller screens */
}
```

# 2. Targeting Tablets:

```css
@media (min-width: 768px) and (max-width: 991px) {
    /* Styles for tablets */
}
```

# 3. Targeting Small to Medium Devices:

```css
@media (max-width: 991px) {
    /* Styles for small to medium devices */
}
```

## 4. Targeting Medium to Large Devices (Desktops, Laptops):

```css
@media (min-width: 992px) {
    /* Styles for medium to large devices (desktops, laptops) */
}
```

## 5. Targeting Landscape Orientation:

```css
@media (orientation: landscape) {
/* Styles for devices in landscape orientation */
}
```

## 6. Targeting Portrait Orientation:

```css
@media (orientation: portrait) {
    /* Styles for devices in portrait orientation */
}
```

## 7. Retina Displays (High Pixel Density):

```css
@media (min-resolution: 2dppx) {
    /* Styles for high pixel density (Retina) displays */
}
```

## 8. Targeting Print Styles:

```css
@media print {
    /* Styles for print layout */
}
```

## 9. Combining Multiple Conditions:

```css
@media (min-width: 768px) and (max-width:
```

```
991px) and (orientation: landscape) {
    /* Styles for tablets in landscape orientation */
    }
    ```
```

These media queries help you tailor the design and layout of your website to ensure optimal presentation on various devices. Depending on your design requirements, you can create additional media queries to cater to specific screen sizes and device characteristics, ensuring a seamless and user-friendly experience across a wide range of devices.

# Making a webpage mobile-friendly

Creating a mobile-friendly webpage involves optimizing the layout, content, and user experience for smaller screens typically found on smartphones and tablets. Here's a step-by-step guide to making your webpage mobile-friendly:
```

# 1. Responsive Design:

- Utilize a responsive design approach using CSS frameworks like Bootstrap or CSS Grid/Flexbox to create layouts that adapt to different screen sizes.
- Set viewport meta tag to ensure proper scaling on mobile devices:

```html
<meta name="viewport" content="width=device-width, initial-scale=1">
```

# 2. Mobile-Optimized Images:

- Use responsive images with the `srcset` attribute to deliver appropriately sized images based on device capabilities and screen sizes.

```html
<img srcset="image-320w.jpg 320w, image-480w.jpg 480w, image-800w.jpg 800w" sizes="(max-width: 320px) 280px,
```

```
(max-width: 480px) 440px, 800px"
          src="image-800w.jpg" alt="Description">
```
```
```

## 3. Readable Text and Font Sizes:

- Ensure text is easily readable on smaller screens by setting appropriate font sizes and line heights.
- Use relative units like `em` or `rem` for font sizes to allow for flexible scaling.

## 4. Touch-Friendly Elements:

- Increase the size of buttons and clickable elements to accommodate finger taps accurately.

## 5. Simplify Navigation:

- Opt for a mobile-friendly navigation pattern, like a hamburger menu, to save space and improve user experience on smaller screens.

## 6. Minimize Load Time:

- Optimize and compress images and other assets to reduce page load time, especially crucial for mobile users.
- Use asynchronous loading for scripts and stylesheets to improve rendering speed.

## 7. Test on Real Devices:

- Test your webpage on various real devices, including smartphones and tablets, to ensure it displays and functions as expected.
- Use browser developer tools to simulate different devices and screen sizes.

## 8. Consistent Experience:

- Maintain a consistent design and user experience across all devices to ensure brand coherence and familiarity.

## 9. Limit Pop-ups and Overlays:

- Avoid excessive pop-ups or overlays that may obstruct the main content or negatively impact the user experience on mobile devices.

## 10. User-Friendly Forms:

- Optimize forms for mobile, utilizing input types suitable for touch, like date pickers or numeric keyboards for numerical input.

## 11. SEO Considerations:

- Ensure your mobile-friendly webpage is SEO optimized for mobile search, following best practices for mobile SEO.

By following these guidelines and best practices, you can create a mobile-friendly webpage that provides an excellent user experience across a variety of devices, ultimately enhancing engagement and usability for your visitors.

# CHAPTER 7:Project: Build a Simple Webpage

Building a simple webpage involves creating the HTML structure for content and using CSS to style it. Here's a basic example of a simple webpage with HTML and CSS:

## 1. HTML (index.html):

```html
<!DOCTYPE html>
<html lang="en">
<head>
    <meta charset="UTF-8">
    <meta name="viewport" content="width=device-width, initial-scale=1.0">
    <title>Simple Webpage</title>
    <link rel="stylesheet" href="styles.css">
</head>
<body>
    <header>
```

```
        <h1>Welcome to My Simple
Webpage</h1>
        </header>

        <main>
        <p>This is a basic example of a
simple webpage.</p>
        <p>Feel free to modify and build
upon it!</p>
        </main>

        <footer>
        <p>&copy; 2023 Simple
Webpage</p>
        </footer>
    </body>
    </html>
    ```
```
```

## 2. CSS (styles.css):

```css
body {
    font-family: Arial, sans-serif;
    margin: 0;
    padding: 20px;
}

header {
    background-color: #f0f0f0;
    padding: 10px;
    text-align: center;
}

main {
    padding: 20px;
}

footer {
    background-color: #f0f0f0;
    padding: 10px;
    text-align: center;
```

```
        position: fixed;
        bottom: 0;
        width: 100%;
    }
    ```
```

**In this example:**

- The HTML file sets up a basic structure with a header, main content, and footer.
- The CSS file (styles.css) provides some minimal styling for the webpage.

You can customize and extend this as per your requirements. To view the webpage, save the HTML in a file named `index.html` and the CSS in a file named `styles.css` in the same directory. Then, open the HTML file in a web browser.

Feel free to add more content, style, and interactivity to make it your own!
```

# Step-by-step guide to creating a basic webpage

Creating a basic webpage involves creating the structure using HTML and styling it with CSS. Here's a step-by-step guide to help you build a simple webpage:

## 1. Set Up the Basic HTML Structure:

Create a new HTML file (e.g., `index.html`) and set up the basic structure using HTML tags.

```html
<!DOCTYPE html>
<html lang="en">
<head>
    <meta charset="UTF-8">
    <meta name="viewport" content="width=device-width, initial-scale=1.0">
    <title>My Basic Webpage</title>
</head>
```

```
<body>
    <!-- Your content goes here -->
</body>
</html>
```
```

## 2. Add Content to the Webpage:

Within the `<body>` tag, add the content you want on your webpage. Use various HTML elements for different types of content like headings, paragraphs, lists, etc.

```html
<body>
    <header>
        <h1>Welcome to My Basic Webpage</h1>
    </header>

    <main>
        <p>This is a simple webpage.</p>
        <p>Here's a list of items:</p>
```
```

```
        <ul>
            <li>Item 1</li>
            <li>Item 2</li>
            <li>Item 3</li>
        </ul>
    </main>


    <footer>
        <p>&copy; 2023 My Basic Webpage</p>
    </footer>
</body>
```
```

## 3. Apply Basic Styling with CSS:

Create a new CSS file (e.g., `styles.css`) to style your webpage. Link this CSS file in the `<head>` section of your HTML.

```html
<head>
    <meta charset="UTF-8">
```
```

```html
    <meta                    name="viewport"
content="width=device-width, initial-scale=1.0">
    <title>My Basic Webpage</title>
    <link rel="stylesheet" href="styles.css">
</head>
```

In `styles.css`, add some basic styles to make your webpage visually appealing.

```css
body {
    font-family: Arial, sans-serif;
    margin: 0;
    padding: 20px;
}

header {
    background-color: #f0f0f0;
    padding: 10px;
    text-align: center;
}
```

```css
main {
    padding: 20px;
}

footer {
    background-color: #f0f0f0;
    padding: 10px;
    text-align: center;
}
```

## 4. Preview Your Webpage:

Save both files (`index.html` and `styles.css`) in the same directory. Open `index.html` in a web browser to see your basic webpage.

## 5. Modify and Enhance:

Customize the content and styles in both HTML and CSS to match your desired design and layout. Experiment with different HTML elements, CSS properties, colors, and layouts to achieve the look you want.

This step-by-step guide provides a foundation for creating a basic webpage. As you become more comfortable, you can explore additional HTML elements, CSS properties, JavaScript for interactivity, and more advanced concepts to enhance your webpage further.

# Incorporating HTML and CSS to style the webpage

Let's build a simple webpage by incorporating HTML for structure and CSS for styling. We'll create a webpage with a header, some content, and a footer.

**1. HTML (index.html):**
```html
<!DOCTYPE html>
<html lang="en">
```

```html
<head>
    <meta charset="UTF-8">
    <meta name="viewport" content="width=device-width, initial-scale=1.0">
    <title>Simple Webpage</title>
    <link rel="stylesheet" href="styles.css">
</head>
<body>
    <header>
        <h1>Welcome to My Simple Webpage</h1>
    </header>

    <main>
        <p>This is a basic example of a simple webpage.</p>
        <p>Feel free to modify and build upon it!</p>
    </main>

    <footer>
        <p>&copy; 2023 Simple Webpage</p>
```

```
    </footer>
</body>
</html>
```

## 2. CSS (styles.css):

```css
body {
    font-family: Arial, sans-serif;
    margin: 0;
    padding: 20px;
    background-color: #f0f0f0;
    color: #333;
}

header {
    background-color: #007BFF;
    padding: 20px;
    text-align: center;
    color: white;
}
```

```css
main {
    padding: 20px;
}

footer {
    background-color: #007BFF;
    padding: 10px;
    text-align: center;
    color: white;
    position: fixed;
    bottom: 0;
    width: 100%;
}
```
```

**In this example:**

- The HTML file (`index.html`) sets up a basic structure with a header, main content, and footer.
- The CSS file (`styles.css`) provides some minimal styling for the webpage.
```

To view the webpage, save the HTML in a file named `index.html` and the CSS in a file named `styles.css`, both in the same directory. Then, open the HTML file in a web browser. Feel free to modify the content and styles to suit your preferences!

# CHAPTER 8:Tips and Best Practices

Absolutely, incorporating best practices is crucial for creating efficient, maintainable, and accessible web content. Here are some tips and best practices for HTML and CSS:

## HTML Best Practices:

### 1. Use Semantic HTML:

Utilize appropriate HTML elements to reflect the structure and meaning of your content. Examples include `<header>`, `<main>`, `<nav>`, `<section>`, and `<footer>`.

### 2. Indentation and Readability:

Maintain consistent indentation and formatting for easy readability and maintenance of your HTML code.

## 3. Comments:

Add comments to explain complex sections or to provide context for future developers who may work on the code.

## 4. Accessibility:

Ensure your HTML is accessible by providing descriptive text through proper usage of `alt` attributes for images, semantic elements, and ARIA attributes where applicable.

## 5. Validation:

Regularly validate your HTML code using online validators to ensure compliance with the HTML specifications and to catch errors.

## 6. Loading Performance:

Load essential resources first and prioritize critical content to improve the perceived speed of your webpage.

# CSS Best Practices:

## 1. Use External CSS:

Externalize your CSS into a separate file to promote code modularity and maintainability.

## 2. Consistent Naming Conventions:

Adopt a consistent naming convention for classes and IDs (e.g., BEM - Block Element Modifier) to make your CSS easier to understand and manage.

## 3. Avoid !important:

Limit the use of `!important` in your styles as it can make debugging and maintaining CSS challenging.

## 4. Responsive Design:

Implement responsive design principles using media queries and relative units like percentages or `em` to ensure your website looks good on various devices.

## 5. Optimize Images:

Compress and optimize images to reduce file sizes and improve page loading speed.

## 6. CSS Reset:

Consider using a CSS reset or normalize to ensure consistent default styles across different browsers.

## 7. Comments:

Add comments to describe the purpose and structure of your CSS code.

## 8. Minify for Production:

Minify your CSS for production to reduce file size and improve page load times.

# General Best Practices:

## 1. Cross-browser Compatibility:

Test your website on multiple browsers and devices to ensure consistent behavior and appearance.

## 2. Version Control:

Use version control systems like Git to keep track of changes, collaborate efficiently, and roll back if needed.

## 3. Learn and Stay Updated:

Continuously learn about new HTML and CSS features, best practices, and evolving web standards to keep your skills up-to-date.

By following these best practices, you'll create clean, maintainable code that performs well and provides a positive user experience. Always prioritize accessibility, responsiveness, and efficiency in your web development projects.

# Proper indentation and code organization

Proper indentation and code organization are essential for writing clean, readable, and maintainable HTML and CSS. They improve collaboration, debugging, and overall code quality. Here are guidelines to achieve this:

## HTML:

### 1. Consistent Indentation:
Use consistent indentation (e.g., 2 or 4 spaces) to clearly show the structure of your HTML elements.

### 2. Nested Elements:
Indent nested elements to reflect their hierarchy within the HTML structure.

```html
<div>
    <p>
```

```
        Nested content.
    </p>
</div>
```

## 3. Line Breaks:

- Use line breaks for each new block or element to enhance readability.

```html
<ul>
    <li>Item 1</li>
    <li>Item 2</li>
</ul>
```

## 4. Attributes:

Format attributes to improve readability, either each on a new line or inline for shorter elements.

```html
<a
    href="https://example.com"
    title="Visit Example"
>
    Visit Example
</a>

<input type="text" name="username" id="username" />
```

## 5. Comments:

Use comments to explain complex sections, important details, or to provide context.

```html
<!-- Header Section -->
<header>
    <h1>Website Title</h1>
</header>
```

# CSS:

## 1. Consistent Indentation:

Indent CSS rules and properties consistently to maintain a clear hierarchy.

```css
body {
    font-family: Arial, sans-serif;
    margin: 0;
    padding: 20px;
}

header {
    background-color: #007BFF;
    padding: 20px;
    text-align: center;
    color: white;
}
```

## 2. Meaningful Ordering:

Arrange CSS properties in a meaningful order (e.g., layout, typography, colors) for better organization and readability.

## 3.Grouping Related Styles:

Group styles that apply to the same element or component together for easier scanning and understanding.

## 4. Comments:

Use comments to describe the purpose or usage of a particular set of styles.

```css
/* Navigation Styles */
nav {
        background-color: #333;
        color: white;
}

/* Button Styles */
```

```
.btn {
    background-color: #007BFF;
    color: white;
}
```
```

## 5. Consistent Naming Conventions:

Follow consistent class and ID naming conventions (e.g., BEM) to maintain uniformity and organization.

## 6. Separate Files for Complex Projects:

For larger projects, consider organizing CSS into separate files based on functionality or components.

# General Tips:

## -Use Tools:

Consider using code editors with built-in features for code formatting, indentation, and syntax highlighting. Extensions like Prettier can help automate code formatting.
```

**Be Consistent:**

Adhere to a consistent coding style and organization throughout your project for easier collaboration and maintenance.

**Review and Refactor:**

Regularly review your code, refactor when necessary, and seek feedback from peers to improve code quality and organization.

By following these guidelines and incorporating good habits, you'll produce well-organized and maintainable HTML and CSS, making it easier for yourself and others to work with the codebase.

# Cross-browser compatibility

Cross-browser compatibility is crucial for ensuring that your website functions and appears consistently across various web browsers. Here are some strategies to achieve better cross-browser compatibility:

## 1. Use Modern Standards and Practices:

- Follow current web standards and best practices to ensure that your website is compatible with modern browsers.

## 2. Test on Multiple Browsers:

- Regularly test your website on different browsers (e.g., Chrome, Firefox, Safari, Edge, Internet Explorer) to identify and address compatibility issues.

## 3. Use Vendor Prefixes:

- For CSS properties that are not fully standardized, use vendor prefixes (-webkit-,

-moz-, -ms-, -o-) to ensure compatibility with different browsers.

```css
.example {
    -webkit-border-radius: 5px;
    -moz-border-radius: 5px;
    border-radius: 5px;
}
```

## 4. Normalize or Reset CSS:

- Use CSS normalization or resetting techniques (e.g., Normalize.css, CSS Reset) to provide a consistent baseline styling across different browsers.

## 5. Feature Detection:

- Use JavaScript feature detection (e.g., `Modernizr`) to apply different code paths based on the capabilities of the user's browser.

```javascript
if (Modernizr.flexbox) {
    // Use flexbox layout
} else {
    // Use alternative layout
}
```

## 6. Polyfills for Missing Features:

- Implement polyfills or shims for missing features in older browsers. These libraries replicate modern functionality in older browsers.

## 7. Use Flexbox and Grid Responsively:

- Leverage CSS Flexbox and Grid Layout in a way that gracefully degrades on browsers that do not support these features.

## 8. Test Early and Often:

- Test your website for cross-browser compatibility during development, not just at the end. This helps catch and address issues early in the development process.

## 9. Keep Abreast of Browser Updates:

- Stay updated with the latest browser versions and updates to ensure your site remains compatible as new features and standards are introduced.

## 10. Responsive Design:

- Employ responsive design principles to ensure your website adapts well to various screen sizes and devices.

## 11. User-Agent Sniffing as a Last Resort:

- Use user-agent sniffing cautiously and only as a last resort, as it's not a recommended approach due to its inaccuracies and potential for misuse.

## 12. Fallbacks for CSS and JavaScript:

- Provide fallbacks or alternative styling/behavior for cases where CSS or JavaScript isn't supported or fails to load.

Remember, achieving perfect cross-browser compatibility is challenging due to the diversity of browsers and versions in use. Aim for a functional and visually acceptable experience on a wide range of modern browsers, focusing on the majority of your target audience. Testing and being proactive in handling compatibility issues are key to success.

# Accessibility considerations

Creating a website that is accessible to all users, including those with disabilities, is not only good practice but often a legal requirement. Here are key accessibility considerations to ensure your website is inclusive and usable by everyone:

# 1. Semantic HTML:

- Use appropriate HTML elements to provide a clear and meaningful structure. Headings, lists, and other semantic elements improve screen reader interpretation and navigation.

# 2. Alternative Text for Images:

- Include descriptive `alt` attributes for images to convey information to users who may not be able to see them. Avoid empty or redundant alt text.

# 3. Keyboard Accessibility:

- Ensure that all functionality is accessible via keyboard navigation. Users should be able to navigate, interact, and submit forms using only the keyboard.

# 4. Focus Styles:

- Clearly indicate focus on links and interactive elements. Use CSS to provide a visible focus indicator to help keyboard users identify where they are on the page.

## 5. Color Contrast:

- Use sufficient color contrast between text and its background to ensure readability for users with visual impairments. The Web Content Accessibility Guidelines (WCAG) provide specific contrast ratios to follow.

## 6. Responsive Design:

- Design your website to be responsive and accessible on various devices and screen sizes, including desktops, tablets, and smartphones.

## 7. Aria Roles and Attributes:

- Use ARIA (Accessible Rich Internet Applications) roles and attributes to enhance the accessibility of complex UI components and dynamic content.

## 8. Form Accessibility:

- Ensure forms are accessible by providing

labels for form controls and using the correct input types. Use ARIA roles for form validation.

## 9. Readable Text:

- Use readable font sizes and styles, and avoid overcrowding the page with too much text. Line height and spacing should enhance readability.

## 10. Video and Audio:

- Provide captions, transcripts, or audio descriptions for multimedia content to make

them accessible to users with hearing impairments.

## 11. Page Structure:

- Use a logical and consistent page structure. Headings should be used in the correct order (h1, h2, h3, etc.) to outline the content hierarchy.

## 12. Error Handling:

- Provide descriptive error messages and suggest possible solutions to users when they encounter form validation errors or other issues.

## 13. Skip to Content Link:

- Include a "skip to content" link at the beginning of the page to allow users to jump directly to the main content, especially helpful for screen reader users.

## 14. Testing and User Feedback:

- Conduct accessibility testing using screen readers and other assistive technologies. Gather feedback from users with disabilities to identify areas for improvement.

## 15. Regular Updates:

- Keep accessibility in mind when adding new features or updating content to ensure ongoing compliance and an inclusive experience for all users.

Adhering to these accessibility considerations will not only make your website more inclusive but also enhance its usability for a broader audience. Always aim for inclusivity in web design to provide an equal and enjoyable experience to everyone.

# CONCLUSION

Creating a website that is accessible, user-friendly, and visually appealing is a multifaceted endeavor. Incorporating best practices in HTML, CSS, cross-browser compatibility, and accessibility is crucial for the success of any web project.

HTML serves as the foundation, providing a structured and semantic layout. Proper indentation and organization enhance readability and maintainability. Semantic elements, alternative text for images, and keyboard accessibility are fundamental considerations that contribute to a more inclusive user experience.

CSS complements HTML, bringing visual aesthetics and layout to the content. Consistent naming conventions, efficient use of CSS selectors, and proper comments enhance code organization and ease of maintenance. Attention to color contrast, responsive design, and graceful degradation ensure a seamless experience across various devices and browsers.

Cross-browser compatibility is essential, considering the diverse browser landscape. Modern standards, feature detection, and graceful fallbacks are strategies that help address disparities and ensure consistency in user experience.

Accessibility is paramount, making the web usable for everyone. Semantic HTML, descriptive text, keyboard accessibility, and testing with assistive technologies are key to creating an inclusive website. Accessibility considerations aren't just about compliance; they're about ensuring that all users can access and interact with your content, regardless of their abilities.

In conclusion, the development of a successful website involves the seamless integration of HTML, CSS, cross-browser compatibility, and accessibility considerations. By adhering to best practices in these areas, we can create web experiences that are not only aesthetically pleasing but also functional and welcoming to all users. Striving for excellence in these aspects is a commitment to creating a more inclusive and user-centric web.